W9-ARH-611

DOWNHILL BMX

BY RAY McCLELLAN

RiverStream Readers

Are you ready to take it to the extreme?

Action Sports HL Readers thrust you into the action-packed world of sports, vehicles, and adventure. These books may include dirt, smoke, fire, and dangerous stunts.

WARNING: Read at your own risk.

RiverStream Publishing reprinted with permission of Bellwether Media Inc.

No part of this publication may be reproduced in whole or in part without written permission of the publisher. For information regarding permission, write to Bellwether Media Inc., Attention: Permissions Department, Post Office Box 19349, Minneapolis, MN 55419.

Library of Congress Cataloging-in-Publication Data

McClellan, Ray.
  Downhill BMX / by Ray McClellan.
      p. cm. -- (Torque : action sports)
  Summary: "Amazing photography accompanies engaging information about downhill BMX. The combination of high-interest subject matter and light text is intended for students in grades 3 through 7"--Provided by publisher.
  Includes bibliographical references and index.
  ISBN-13: 978-1-60014-139-3 (hardcover : alk. paper)
  ISBN-10: 1-60014-139-0 (hardcover : alk. paper)
  1. Bicycle motocross--Juvenile literature. 2. Extreme sports--Juvenile literature. I. Title.

  GV1049.3.M424 2008
  796.6'2--dc22
                                                                    2007042405

1 2 3 4 5 CG 16 15 14 13
RiverStream Publishing—Corporate Graphics, Mankato, MN—122013—1038CGW13

CONTENTS

WHAT IS DOWNHILL BMX?

BMX downhill riders sprint down steep dirt slopes. They soar shoulder-to-shoulder over breathtaking jumps. A BMX downhill race is a high-speed, high-flying battle for first place.

BMX grew out of the sport of **motocross**. In motocross, motorcycle racers speed around dirt tracks and over jumps. Bicycle riders wanted to have the same intense fun as motocross riders. The result was the invention of BMX, short for bicycle motocross. The first BMX races were on classic oval tracks with jumps and turns. Some riders wanted to experience higher speeds, bigger air, and bigger thrills. They started BMX racing on downhill courses. Downhill BMX is now the fastest and most exciting form of BMX racing.

fast fact

Scot Breithaupt started the first official BMX organization in 1970. He called it Bicycle United Motocross Society, or BUMS.

DOWNHILL BMX EQUIPMENT

BMX racing bikes are built to be fast and easy to control. They have small frames that ride low to the ground. Frames are made of steel or **aluminum**. The wheels are 20 or 24 inches (50.8 or 60.9 centimeters) in **diameter**.

Most BMX bikes have only one **gear**. Many do not have **suspension systems**. This helps reduce the bike's weight. It also means that the rider is not cushioned from bumps and rough landings.

Good **traction** is necessary for racing on rough surfaces. BMX downhill riders use fat, knobby tires. These give the best grip on dirt and mud.

Safety is important to BMXers. Full-face helmets are required. A fall from a speeding bike can be dangerous. Knee and elbow pads, long-sleeved shirts, long pants, and gloves help protect a rider who takes a spill.

DOWNHILL BMX IN ACTION

BMX downhill races are full of excitement. A pack of riders starts out together at the top. Riders can reach speeds of 70 miles (113 kilometers) per hour on the steepest sections. Runs also include some uphill sections to test the endurance of riders. Sharp banks help riders take tight turns. Their bikes may get almost horizontal while they maneuver a turn.

Step-downs are a course's biggest challenge. A step-down is a sudden drop-off. It can be a drop of up to 40 feet (12.2 meters). Riders may not even see the landing until they are in the air. Skilled riders have been known to pass others in mid-air.

BMX downhill riders can compete all over the country. Riders compete according to skill and age classes. Riders as young as three and older than 70 have competed. Each competition has a series of heats called **motos**. The winner of each moto races in the championship. The championship race is called the **main**. Up to eight riders race in the main. Every BMX rider wants to be the first one across the finish line.

GLOSSARY

aluminum—a lightweight metal used for making bike frames

diameter—the distance across a circle

gear—a set of wheels with teeth; gears turn and transfer power from the person pedaling to the wheels.

main—the final heat in a BMX racing competition

moto—a qualifying heat in a BMX racing competition

motocross—a sport in which riders drive motorcycles around dirt courses featuring sharp turns and huge jumps

step-down—a sudden drop-off in a BMX downhill course

suspension system—the system of springs and shock absorbers that connect the frame to the wheels in some bikes

traction—the grip of the tires on a riding surface

TO LEARN MORE

AT THE LIBRARY
David, Jack. *BMX Racing*. Minneapolis, Minn.:
Bellwether, 2008.

Fiske, Brian. *BMX Bikes: Design and Equipment*.
Mankato, Minn.: Capstone, 2004.

McClellan, Ray. *BMX Freestyle*. Minneapolis,
Minn.: Bellwether, 2008.

ON THE WEB
Learning more about downhill BMX
is as easy as 1, 2, 3.

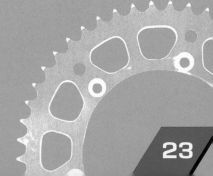

1. Go to www.factsurfer.com
2. Enter "downhill BMX" into search box.
3. Click the "Surf" button and you will see a list
   of related web sites.

With factsurfer.com, finding more
information is just a click away.

INDEX

The images in this book are reproduced through the courtesy of: Jeff Sack/Shazamm/ESPN Images, front cover, pp. 3, 8-9, 11, 18 (top), 19; Tony Donaldson/Shazamm/ESPN Images, pp. 4-5, 12, 20; R. Archer/ Shazamm/ESPN Images, p. 6; Phil Walter/Getty Images, p. 7; Redline, p. 10; Steve Buddendeck/Sha- zamm/ESPN Images, p. 13; Robert Laberge/Getty Images, p. 14; Fox Head Inc., p. 15 (top); Juan Marti- nez, p. 15 (bottom); Pat Little/Associated Press, pp. 16, 18 (bottom); ESPN Images, p. 17; Chris Hallman/ Shazamm/ESPN Images, p. 21.